Contents

New words

1982 **2019**

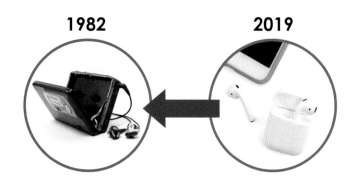

years ago

ancient
(adjective)

asteroid

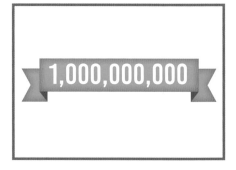

billion

dinosaur

evolve

feather

forest

life

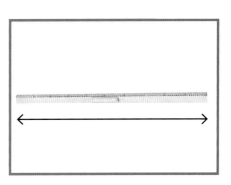

metre

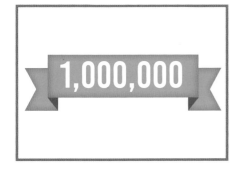

million

rock

What are the oldest animals?

Earth is about 4.6 **billion** years old! **Life** began in Earth's seas about 3.7 billion **years ago**.

The first plants **evolved** about 900 **million** years ago, and the first animals evolved about 890 million years ago.

fossil

We learn about **ancient** animals from fossils.

6

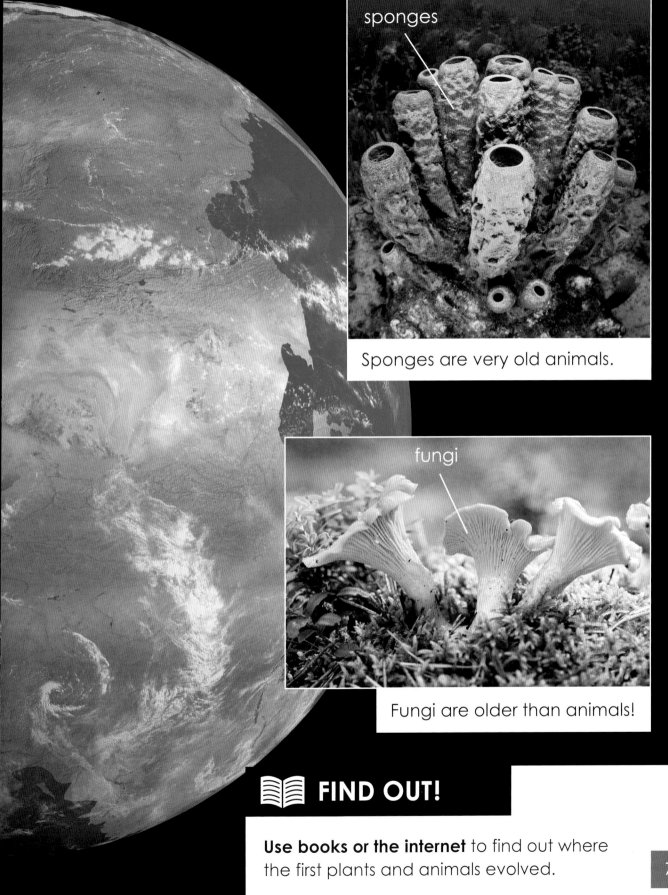

sponges

Sponges are very old animals.

fungi

Fungi are older than animals!

📖 **FIND OUT!**

Use books or the internet to find out where
the first plants and animals evolved.

What was the Cambrian explosion?

Look at these interesting animals from the Cambrian explosion! The Cambrian explosion was a time when many new animals evolved in Earth's seas. It started about 530 million years ago and took 13 to 25 million years to end.

trilobite

Trilobites evolved in the Cambrian explosion and lived for about 270 million years.

Hurdia victoria evolved in the Cambrian explosion and was one of the first animals to eat other animals.

Hurdia victoria

PROJECT

Work with a friend. Make a poster about some of the different animals from the Cambrian explosion.

What lived in ancient seas?

Some of the sea animals
millions of years ago were very big.
The biggest sea animals were the ichthyosaurs.
Shastasaurus was an ichthyosaur.
Shastasaurus could be 21 **metres** long
and lived 210 million years ago.

ichthyosaur

flipper

Plesiosaurus used flippers to move in the sea.

Pliosaurus had lots of big teeth.

Look at Helicoprion's mouth!

 **THINK!**

Can you see these animals in the sea today?

How big were dinosaurs?

We often think of **dinosaurs** as very big animals, but not all dinosaurs were big.

Epidexipteryx lived about 160 million years ago and was only 44 centimetres long! It was like a bird, but it could not fly. One of the biggest dinosaurs was Argentinosaurus. It was 40 metres long and 21 metres tall!

Epidexipteryx had beautiful tail **feathers**.

tail feathers

Argentinosaurus didn't eat other animals.

▶ **WATCH!**

Watch the video (see page 32).
How big are the baby dinosaurs?

Did dinosaurs have feathers?

Yutyrannus huali was a dinosaur with feathers, but it didn't have wings. Its feathers helped to keep it warm and they stopped it from getting wet.

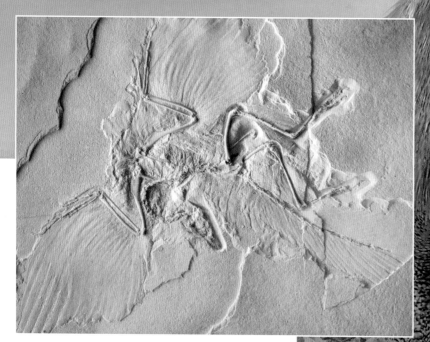

People found the first fossil of a dinosaur with feathers in 1996.

Yutyrannus
huali

Birds evolved from dinosaurs.
Many dinosaurs had feathers,
but not all dinosaurs with
feathers could fly.

Maybe Tyrannosaurus rex
had feathers, too!

THINK!

What do birds use their feathers for?

Where did dinosaurs live?

The first dinosaurs lived on a very hot Earth about 235 million years ago. They lived in the desert and weren't very big. Then Earth changed and lots of plants grew. The big dinosaurs evolved and lived in many places – **forests**, mountains, and next to the sea and rivers.

desert

There were dinosaurs on Earth for 170 million years.

Spinosaurus lived in swamps.

swamp

Stegosaurus lived in forests.

📖 **FIND OUT!**

Use books or the internet to find out where your favourite dinosaur lived.

What did dinosaurs eat?

We often think of dinosaurs as big animals that eat smaller animals. But most dinosaurs ate plants. Some of the plant-eating dinosaurs were very big, but they moved slowly. The meat-eating dinosaurs ate other animals and had strong teeth.

Ankylosaurus was a plant-eating dinosaur.

Allosaurus was a meat-eating dinosaur.

Alamosaurus

Caudipteryx

Some dinosaurs ate plants and meat.

🔍 LOOK!

Look at the pages. Why would some plant-eating dinosaurs be big?

19

Where did dinosaurs go?

Most of the dinosaurs died about 66 million years ago. People think that they died because a big **asteroid** hit Earth. This changed the weather, and plants died. Plant-eating dinosaurs died and meat-eating dinosaurs had nothing to eat. Then they died, too.

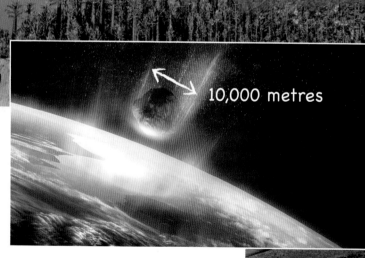

10,000 metres

The asteroid was very big.

There is a crater in Mexico from 66 million years ago.

crater

▶ WATCH!

Watch the video (see page 32).
What happened to the dinosaurs after the asteroid hit Earth?

How big was a woolly mammoth?

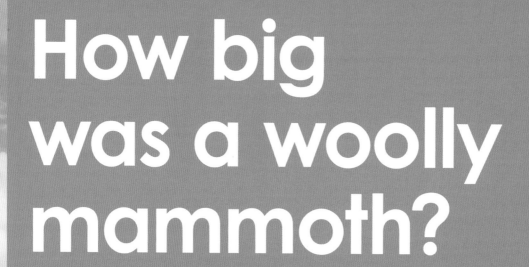

Woolly mammoths lived on Earth for about 800,000 years, but they all died about 4,500 years ago.

Mammoths lived in cold places and had lots of hair on their bodies to keep them warm. Some mammoths were very big. The biggest mammoths grew to about 4 metres tall!

mammoth

4 metres

elephant

Mammoths and elephants evolved from the same animal.

Ancient people drew pictures of mammoths.

 **PROJECT**

Work with a friend. Find out about the woolly mammoth and make a poster about it.

23

What is a fossil?

Fossils are very old **rocks** with ancient life in them. Some fossils were the bones or shells of animals. Some fossils are pictures in rock. The fossils show us plants and animals from the past. Fossils can be millions or billions of years old! We learn about ancient life from fossils.

This fossil is a dragonfly in amber.

We learned about the sabre-toothed cat from fossils.

We learned about the Basilosaurus from fossils.

🔍 LOOK!

Look at the pages. What different fossils can you see?

What is a palaeontologist?

Would you like to learn about dinosaurs for your job? That is what a palaeontologist does! Palaeontologists study plants and animals that lived millions of years ago. They find and study fossils to understand more about ancient animals.

Palaeontologists found this big ichthyosaur fossil in 2021.

Palaeontologists found this dinosaur fossil in America. The dinosaur died when the asteroid hit Earth about 66 million years ago!

▶ **WATCH!**

Watch the video (see page 32).
Would you like this job? Why or why not?

Where can we see fossils?

Palaeontologists find lots of fossils, but where can you see them?

You can see the fossils of trilobites, ichthyosaurs, dinosaurs, mammoths and many more ancient plants and animals in museums.

You can find fossils on some beaches.

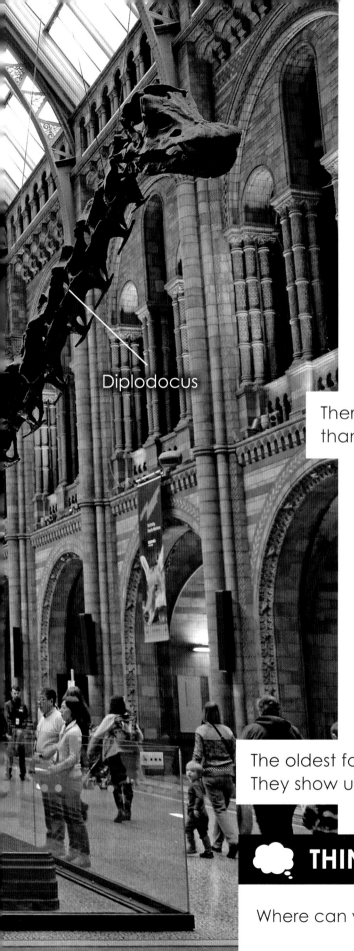

Diplodocus

There are dinosaur fossils that are more than 100 million years old in museums!

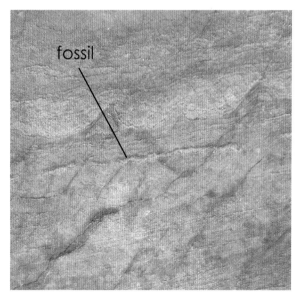

fossil

The oldest fossils are about 3.7 billion years old. They show us the first life on Earth.

 **THINK!**

Where can you see fossils near your home?

Quiz

Choose the correct answers.

1 Animals evolved about . . . years ago.
   a 700 million
   b 890 million
   c 3.7 billion

2 The biggest sea animal was the . . .
   a Helicoprion.
   b Plesiosaurus.
   c ichthyosaurs.

3 The first dinosaurs lived on a . . . Earth.
   a cold
   b hot
   c small

4 Most dinosaurs ate . . .
   a plants.
   b meat.
   c plants and meat.

5 Dinosaurs died when . . . hit Earth.
  a a fossil
  b an asteroid
  c a shell

6 All mammoths died about . . . years ago.
  a 4,500,000,000
  b 4,500,000
  c 4,500

7 . . . are very old rocks with ancient life in them.
  a Fossils
  b Feathers
  c Dodos

8 A palaeontologist studies . . .
  a volcanoes.
  b asteroids.
  c ancient animals.

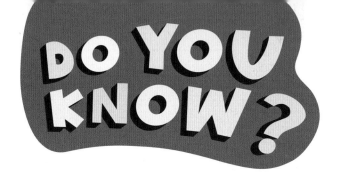

DO YOU KNOW?

Visit www.ladybirdeducation.co.uk for
FREE DO YOU KNOW? teaching resources.

- video clips with simplified voiceover and subtitles
- video and comprehension activities
- class projects and lesson plans
- audio recording of every book
- digital version of every book
- full answer keys

To access video clips, audio tracks and digital books:

1 Go to **www.ladybirdeducation.co.uk**
2 Click 'Unlock book'
3 Enter the code below

sBfgnfW8OB

Stay safe online! Some of the DO YOU KNOW? activities ask children to do extra research online. Remember:

- ensure an adult is supervising;
- use established search engines such as Google or Kiddle;
- children should never share personal details, such as name, home or school address, telephone number or photos.